Discovering
Nature

Mason Crest

THE GREAT OUTDOORS!

Camping

Discovering Nature

Fishing

Hiking and Backpacking

Horseback Riding

Hunting

Mountain Biking

Snow Sports

Survival Skills

Water Sports

THE GREAT OUTDOORS! →

Discovering Nature

DIANE BAILEY

MC

Mason Crest
450 Parkway Drive, Suite D
Broomall, PA 19008
www.masoncrest.com

Printed and bound in the United States of America.

Series ISBN: 978-1-4222-3565-2
Hardback ISBN: 978-1-4222-3567-6
EBook ISBN: 978-1-4222-8312-7

First printing
1 3 5 7 9 8 6 4 2

Produced by Shoreline Publishing Group LLC
Santa Barbara, California
Editorial Director: James Buckley Jr.
Designer: Patty Kelley
Production: Sandy Gordon
www.shorelinepublishing.com

Cover photographs by Starletdarlene/Dreamstime.com.

Names: Bailey, Diane, 1966-
Title: Discovering nature / by Diane Bailey.
Description: Broomall, PA : Mason Crest, [2017] | Series: The great
        outdoors | Includes index.
Identifiers: LCCN 2016002435| ISBN 9781422235676 (hardback) | ISBN
        9781422235652 (series) | ISBN 9781422283127 (ebook)
Subjects: LCSH: Natural history--Juvenile literature.
Classification: LCC QH48 .B245 2017 | DDC 508--dc23
LC record available at http://lccn.loc.gov/2016002435

CONTENTS

Introduction: Discover Nature! 6

Chapter 1: Into the Great Outdoors! 10

Chapter 2: Getting It Done Right 16

Chapter 3: Get Great Gear 26

Chapter 4: Further Adventures 36

Find Out More. 46

Series Glossary of Key Terms 47

Index/Author 48

KEY ICONS TO LOOK FOR

Words to Understand: These words with their easy-to-understand definitions will increase the reader's understanding of the text, while building vocabulary skills.

Sidebars: This boxed material within the main text allows readers to build knowledge, gain insights, explore possibilities, and broaden their perspectives by weaving together additional information to provide realistic and holistic perspectives.

Research Projects: Readers are pointed toward areas of further inquiry connected to each chapter. Suggestions are provided for projects that encourage deeper research and analysis.

Text-Dependent Questions: These questions send the reader back to the text for more careful attention to the evidence presented here.

Series Glossary of Key Terms: This back-of-the-book glossary contains terminology used throughout this series. Words found here increase the reader's ability to read and comprehend higher-level books and articles in this field.

Educational Videos: Readers can view videos by scanning our QR codes, providing them with additional educational content to supplement the text. Examples include news coverage, moments in history, speeches, iconic sports moments and much more!

Delias mysis onca
Pieridae

Graphium agamemnon *gatum
Papilionidae

Hypolimnas bolina
Nymphalidae

Psychonotis ca
Lycae

Papilio olysses a
Papilionidae

Cirrochroa regina
Nymphalidae

Graphium sarpedon choredon
Papilionidae

Phalanta alcippe cervina
Nymphalidae

Dichorragia nin
Nymphalidae

ra polydorus
apilionidae

Arhopala azenia
Lycaenidae

Jamides nemophilus nemophilus
Lycaenidae

andaca b
Pieridae

Triodes priamus
Papilionidae

Graphium weiskei
Papilionidae

Graphium aristeus pa
Papilionidae

Pantoporia venilia
Nymphalidae

inca lurgis
Nymph lidae

Tae
N

Discover Nature!

 n the way home from the dentist one day, Frances Hamerstrom's babysitter took her to the natural history museum. Frances was fascinated by the cases full of insects. Each one was carefully labeled with its official Latin name. At home, Frances had six shoeboxes full of dead insects. Unfortunately, she only had one small guidebook to help her identify them. Here were the answers she wanted! Frances read through the labels, trying to remember everything. She did not have enough time to find out everything she wanted to know. She needed an excuse to go back. In her mind, that meant another trip to the dentist. Frances was ready to do whatever was needed. Finally, she convinced her mother to take her back to the natural history museum.

Frances was always interested in discovering more about nature. As a child, she took in wild animals and kept them as pets. She made secret hiding places in the tops of trees. She made "bedrooms" under their branches and slept there. She planted poison ivy near her garden so no one would bother her there.

Frances grew up to be a famous naturalist. Her research on the prairie chicken in Wisconsin helped save it from extinction. Her interest in nature, though, started with just a few trips outside her house. The land near her home remains a wildlife preserve today, thanks in large part to her efforts.

The greater prairie chicken was saved thanks to Hamerstrom's efforts.

Step one to discovering nature: Get outside and explore . . . bring friends!

She also explored the Amazon and other parts of the world. But she always came home to the house where she lived for more than 50 years. It did not have running water and hadn't been painted since the Civil War. But for her, it was the center of a larger, wilder world. Every day, she explored the land nearby, always discovering new things about nature.

It doesn't really matter what's outside your home—nature is everywhere. Your explorations could start on your porch, on the lawn, or in an alley in a city. Wherever you go, nature is already there. Like Frances, you just have to notice it.

📖 WORDS TO UNDERSTAND

botanist a type of scientist who studies plants

evolution a scientific theory that explains how animals adapt to their environments and change over time

habitat the places where certain species live

photosynthesis the process plants use to turn sunlight into food and energy

taxonomy the system used to classify plant and animal species

CHAPTER 1

Into the Great Outdoors!

Keeping the Earth running properly is a big project. Nature is forever doing one thing or another in this endless job. Birds sing to attract mates. Squirrels scramble along the tops of fences and dash in front of cars as they collect nuts for the winter. Leaves fall off trees and break down to put nutrients back in the soil. Sometimes nature has a task that is steady and quiet, like the **photosynthesis** of a plant. Other times her job is sudden and loud, like a hurricane hurtling across the ocean. She may take thousands of years for waves to pound rocks into tiny grains of sand. Or she may just need a moment for a bolt of lightning to start a fire that burns millions of acres. Big or small, each thing influences everything else. Best of all, it is all on display—for us.

Taking Notice

Thousands of years ago, people were more in touch with nature than they are now. They had to know about nature just to survive. By observing the lifestyles of animals, they figured out the best ways to hunt. They figured out how to protect themselves from predators. They learned which trees had good, hard wood for building shelters. They learned which berries and mushrooms were safe to eat, and which ones were poisonous. They observed processes and noticed patterns. Then they passed the information along to later generations.

Most of these early naturalists were just ordinary people. They learned about nature because it helped them in their own lives. However, there have also been some important naturalists whose work has had a larger effect. One was the Swedish **botanist** Carl Linnaeus. In the 1700s, he worked to classify plants and animals based on their characteristics. This is known as **taxonomy**. The system invented by Linnaeus is still used today.

You might have heard of Meriwether Lewis and William Clark. They were famous American explorers who traveled across the American West from 1804 to 1806. Lewis and Clark were also naturalists. They took notes on everything they encountered. They recorded the locations of rivers and mountains. They wrote down the kinds of plants and animals they saw. Their work helped people understand the natural world in the United States.

Lewis and Clark led the way west as naturalists and explorers.

By the late 1800s, more people were looking at nature on a large scale. They started to realize that people could have a huge effect on what happened in nature. It was not always good. During the Industrial Revolution of the late 1800s, factories pumped tons of polluted air into the environment. Ancient trees were cut down for lumber to make everything from houses to tooth-picks. This destroyed habitats for many birds and animals. These kinds of problems motivated people to try to prevent damage. It was the beginning of the environmental movement.

Another very influential naturalist was the Englishman Charles Darwin. In the 1830s, Darwin sailed around the world for five years. Along the way, he studied all kinds of plants and animals. Darwin is best known for proposing a theory of **evolution**. Evolution describes how species adapt to their environments and gradually change as a result. As a working naturalist, Darwin noticed the similarities and differences between species and wondered how they had occurred.

Starting Out

 f you want to discover nature, it is not necessary to take to the high seas as Charles Darwin did. You do not have to blaze a trail to the West like Lewis and Clark. Instead, some of the best training is to learn to recognize what is happening right under your nose.

Discovering nature starts with small steps and short trips. You might spend half an hour in your backyard garden, tracking the path of an in-sect. You could take a survey of the trees around your house, counting and identifying them. You might keep a record of the weather, and see how it affects the behavior of animals.

It's easy to read a field guide that will tell you what plants and an-imals live in what places. The TV news will tell you how many inches of snow there were. But that's the easy way out—and it's not nearly as

Be a Backyard Naturalist

fun. Making a point to notice things for yourself puts you in touch with what is happening around you. That's an important part of building your skills as a naturalist.

You can move from your backyard to a nearby park, a patch of woods, or even an overgrown parking lot. Every area has something to discover. Try to observe different types of **habitats**, such as woods or open grasslands. Look at the differences between puddles and ponds. A general nature walk can help you get the lay of the land. Then, once you've been out a few times, give yourself a specific goal. Maybe you will see how many different types of pine cones you can find, or how many bird calls you can identify.

It takes patience to be a good naturalist. Discovering nature isn't all sunny walks in the park. Nature is doing her thing everywhere, all the time. If you want to see the show, you're probably going to get dirt under your fingernails and snow down your boots. Bugs will bite you, and the pollen might make you sneeze. Sometimes you'll be too hot or too cold.

And then something will make it all worth it. What will it be?

That's what you have to find out!

 ## HUMAN NATURE

Most people think of nature as being everything except themselves. In fact, people are just as much a part of nature as everything else. After all, it's called "human" nature! It may not seem very exciting to watch people cross the street, or shop for groceries, or sit in class. However, there may be interesting patterns if you look closely. Who waits for the light to change, and who runs across as soon as the traffic clears? Pick a couple sections of the store and "spy" on the people who shop there. Do they spend more time shopping for chips or chicken? Who focuses on their work, and who looks out the window, ready to go outside? People-watching can tell you a lot about nature—your own!

Find ways to discover nature, from the smallest bugs to the biggest trees.

TEXT-DEPENDENT QUESTIONS

1. How did Carl Linnaeus contribute to the study of the natural world?

2. Why did the environmental movement start?

3. What are two simple ways you could start to observe nature around your home?

RESEARCH PROJECT

Look into the lives of several famous naturalists, and list some of their important contributions. How did they build upon each other's work?

biodiversity the amount of variety in plants and animals in a particular area

ecosystem the habitats of species and the ways that species interact with each other

nocturnal active at night instead of daytime

CHAPTER 2

Getting It Done Right

ometimes you just need to charge right into something. Your chores. A game of basketball. A big project for school. Nature, however, is better used for *recharging*. It is better to try to be quiet and "invisible" when you are out in nature. You will not be as likely to disturb things around you, and will have the best chance to observe it.

Habitats and Ecosystems

ome places get a lot of attention. Scientists spend a lot of time studying the coral reefs off the coast of Australia. They want to know about the tropical rainforests in the Amazon Basin in Brazil. These places have a lot of **biodiversity**. They are fascinating to observe.

Even a springtime walk in the woods can led to discoveries.

Where Animals Live

However, the "interesting" things are not all happening in the oceans or the rainforests. The small things going on near your home are just as important. Nature is all connected. As a naturalist, you can begin by understanding what is happening in your neck of the woods (or grass, or desert). This will help you understand what is happening far away.

All species of animals and plants have places they like to live—their habitats. They can be large or small. No matter where you live, there are dozens of habitats around you. The garden in your backyard could be considered a habitat. The stream just beyond your fence is another one. What about the fence itself? Lots of animals like to nest or burrow around the protected area of a fence. Habitats change all the time. A drainage ditch that is regularly filled with running water in the spring may be completely dried out by the summer. The species that lived there either die or move elsewhere. New species move in.

The boundaries between habitats are particularly interesting to observe. The edges of habitats are like nature's malls. They are more varied, so they attract more types of plants and animals. Here, animals can "shop" for the necessities of life. Birds can collect bits of dry grass or twigs for their nests. Mice can forage for seeds to eat. If there are mice around, then snakes will probably show up, too. They want the mice for *their* dinner.

Of course, many species live in the same place. They interact with each other and with their habitats in countless ways. Put all these species and their actions together, and you have described an **ecosystem**. An ecosystem is more than the plants and animals in a habitat. It also includes how everything works together. For example, fish and algae may both live in a pond. The fact that the fish eat the algae is an important part of the ecosystem.

 CLOSE TO HOME

Nature is a great guest—and she hardly ever refuses an invitation to visit. It's easy to bring nature close to your home. You could start by letting your garden or a corner of the yard get a little overgrown. Nature does not care if the lawn is mowed—in fact, you're more likely to get some action if the grass is taller and a few weeds have crept in. You can also plant shrubs or flowers that are attractive to certain animals such as butterflies or rabbits. Animals are always on the lookout for water, so a birdbath is a sure way to draw visitors. Add a bird feeder, and you'll attract a variety of birds—and probably other animals—who may go to battle for a chance at the food.

Keeping Watch

ature is always changing, so seeing a place in one visit won't give the full picture. Pick a place that you can return to on a regular basis. Try to go at different times of day, and in different types of weather. Involve all five of your senses. People evolved in nature, and we are set up to see it, hear it, smell it, touch it, and taste it. (Be careful with that last one, though. Lots of plants are poisonous!) It's interesting to try to isolate each of your senses. As a species, humans are extremely dependent on eyesight, but it cannot tell us everything. What happens when you close your eyes and focus only on what you can hear or smell? When you do open your eyes, remember that nature does not happen only at eye level. There are hundreds of things happening over your head and under your feet.

CHANGING OF THE GUARD

Just before sunrise and just after sunset are nature's rush hours. These are busy times with a lot of interesting things to watch. After the sun goes down—but before it gets completely dark—rabbits and birds scrounge around for the day's last meal before they settle in for the night. As they are

on their way home, they will pass **nocturnal** animals such as raccoons, frogs, bats, and owls. They have spent the day under cover and are just waking up. Insects such as mosquitoes and crickets also tend to come out at night. Another busy time is at dawn, when the night shift goes home and the daytime animals head out. As the saying goes, the early bird gets the worm, so it's good to be first in line.

Find a place in nature you feel comfortable, and drink it in!

Not all of nature is alive. Climate and weather, for example, have huge effects on what is going on. Humans can go inside when the weather gets nasty, but plants and animals have to take what nature dishes out. How do they adapt? The geography of an area is also critical. Are there a lot of hills or is it flat? Rocky or sandy? Wet or dry? All of this affects the lifestyles of nature's species.

Observing plants and animals takes different skills. Plants are easier in a way because they stay in one place. You don't have to chase after them! However, they tend to change slowly, so it is necessary to be patient. Plan to invest some time and look for changes over several days or months. For example, you might keep a record of when different types of trees lose their leaves in the fall or leaf out again in the spring. If you have a garden, you could measure the growth of different types of plants. What sprouts first? What grows fastest?

Observing animals is a little trickier. Most wild animals want nothing to do with humans. They feel threatened if people get too near. Then they will run away—or fly, or slither, or swim—to safety. This does not mean that animals are impossible to observe. They are similar to people in a lot of ways. They want to be where they are safe and comfortable. It is a top priority for them to have enough food. Places with more food and water are more likely to have animals. If there is a lack of food, water, or shelter, animals may only pass through briefly.

Make a Record

To help you remember what you observe, always carry a notebook and a pencil. Get in the habit of taking notes on what you observe. Practice making sketches, too, even if you take pictures. With a sketch you can emphasize different things. You can also jot down notes on your drawing. These are like captions that will help you remember later what you saw. Once you get home, while your mind is still fresh, add in other details. What patterns did you notice? Did anything seem odd or out of place?

Photographs are another way to help you keep a record of what you observed. Getting good photographs or videos begins before you leave the house. Perhaps you want to get pictures of a particular type of bird. Before you go out, do some research to find out where you will be likely to find it. Check the weather. If it is raining or overcast, there will not be as much light. Wooded areas or closed-in spaces (like holes) will also be darker. This will make it harder to get a good picture. Animals are always on the move, so it can be challenging to get a clear, focused photograph. Be patient. Wait until animals pause to sniff the air or grab a drink. That's a good time to get a shot. Don't take the same picture over and over again. Photograph things from different angles. You might want to get an overall picture, and then more detailed pictures of different parts. Finally, try photographing the same thing at different times of day, over the course of several days, or even an entire season.

The "macro" setting on your camera will help you take closeups.

Naming Names

One of a naturalist's jobs is to identify different things in the environment. This includes the land itself, including rocks, soil, and water. It also includes the different kinds of plants and animals that live there. The point of identifying a species, though, is not simply to know its name. That is not much use by itself. Instead, once you know the name of something, you can research it further to find out what its role in the environment is.

Field guides can help when you are trying to identify what's what. However, there are millions of different types of species. It is necessary to observe a few key characteristics and then go from there. It is like a very complex matching game! Here are some ideas of where to start:

Trees, Plants, and Flowers

- What is the overall height and thickness of the tree or plant?
- Where does it grow? In an open space or with a cluster of other trees or flowers? In a wet area or a dry one?
- What is the color and texture of the bark?
- What is the color, texture, and shape of the leaves?
- Is there a distinctive smell?
- What animals or birds live nearby?

Animals

- How large is it? What is its shape?
- What color or markings does it have?
- What kinds of sounds does it make?
- What is its habitat?
- Look for tracks and scat (poop). The shape and size of footprints and scat can help identify what animals have been around.

This list just scratches the surface. Depending on what you are trying to identify, you may come up with other questions. However, the principles of identification are still the same. Observe what something looks, sounds, or smells like. Take note of its behavior (if any), and other physical characteristics. Notice the details of the habitat. This includes where you found it, and what other plants or animals are nearby. Many species appear similar, but with practice you will know how to pin down the small details that make them different.

Expand on your memories by keeping notes of your discoveries in a journal.

TEXT-DEPENDENT QUESTIONS

1. How is an ecosystem different from a habitat?

2. Why are sunrise and sunset good times to observe nature?

3. What are two tips to remember when taking photographs of plants and animals in the wild?

RESEARCH PROJECT

There are millions of species of plants and animals in the world, and more are being discovered all the time. Research the process scientists and naturalists use to identify new species. Find the names of some recently "discovered" animals.

WORDS TO UNDERSTAND

camouflage a pattern or disguise in clothing designed to make it blend into the surroundings

scalpel a small, sharp blade

traction the ability of a material to hold onto, or grip, another surface

CHAPTER 3

Get Great Gear

Getting out in nature is simple. Open the door, step outside, and boom! You're there. Discovering what is around you does not require much equipment, either. The most important tools are your brain and your body. However, there are some pieces of gear that will make your job a little easier.

Dressing for the Outdoors

Plants and animals are always doing battle with one another. As a result, they have developed a lot of ways to protect themselves. Some are merely irritating to humans, such as itching from poison ivy. Others can be a lot more dangerous, like the bite of a poisonous snake. A few precautions will make your outings more enjoyable.

The first line of defense is clothing. In general, it is a good idea to wear long pants and long sleeves. These will protect your skin from sunburn, insect bites, and plants that might give you a rash. Lightweight but sturdy fabrics such as cotton or linen will stay cool in summer, as will synthetics made for the outdoors. Wool is a good choice for winter, especially if you plan to be out in snow or rain. Wool absorbs moisture and pulls it away from the skin. This helps your body hold in heat. A waterproof winter coat is also helpful.

A **camouflage** pattern will help you blend in if you want to stay hidden, but this is usually not necessary. Just try to stay away from bright

Outerwear of manmade materials works better in most weathers.

When facing snow or ice, make sure your boots have good tread.

colors. These tend to attract insects. They may also scare away other animals who know that these colors are not part of their natural habitat. It's always nice to have pockets in your pants or jacket to keep supplies handy. Take a pair of gloves to protect your hands.

Sandals might be okay for the backyard or the beach. For places with a lot of undergrowth, choose boots or close-toed shoes. Nature is full of itchy, sticky things lurking underfoot. Sneakers are comfortable, but they often do not have a lot of traction for rough or slippery places. Also, the sides are soft, so it is easier to get hurt on sharp rocks or branches. Wear something sturdy that has a hard sole with good traction. Tuck the bottoms of your pants inside your boots or shoes—that discourages insects and spiders from getting in.

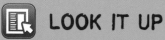
Nature is big and complicated. No one person can understand it without a little help. That's what field guides are for! There are informational guides on virtually every aspect of nature. They can help you figure out what you are seeing or hearing. A pile of books on every topic will get pretty heavy to carry along when you are out in the field, so plan ahead to make your outing focus on something in particular. Then choose a few pocket guides that you can easily take along. Many smartphone apps are available with the same or similar information as field guides. At home, you can refer to more detailed books or look things up on the Internet.

Bug spray is a must-have for many people. Woods and moist areas have the most insects. Just don't spray your hands, as you may forget and touch your nose or face. Bug sprays are generally safe on the skin, but they should not get inside your body. And don't forget to use sunscreen whenever the sun is out.

Stocking the Backpack

or the most part, you do not need sophisticated tools to discover nature. However, a few key supplies will make things easier and more productive.

Nature happens far and wide. It also happens up close and personal. Improve your vision with a pair of binoculars and a magnifying glass. Many animals will take off when people get too close, but observing them through binoculars allows you to watch from far away. They won't be bothered, and this will help keep you safe from a possible animal attack. A magnifying glass will help you examine tiny insects. It can be a great tool for detecting patterns in leaves, as well. Take along a flashlight for night explorations or for looking in holes or tree trunks.

Several items will help if you plan to collect specimens. A butterfly net can aid in collecting butterflies, moths, and other flying insects. Tweezers are good for picking up insects and other small items. If your specimens are alive, you want to keep them that way. Avoid keeping animals until they die. Either prepare a way to take care of them at home, or study them quickly and then release them back into the habitat you found them in. It is possible to buy containers specially designed to house small animals or insects, but jars or plastic containers with lids will also work. Make

A small pair of binoculars is a great way to get closeup looks at birds.

sure to punch holes in the lid to let air circulate. Add a little water and a leaf or two in case your critter gets the munchies.

Finally, don't forget to take care of yourself. Bring food and water even if you are planning a short trip. There's always the possibility of an emergency or accident. An energy bar and extra bottle of water can keep you going for a while.

Bringing it Home

Observing nature is one thing. Making sense out of it is quite another. After a day out in the field, you may have collected a lot of specimens. You might have a couple of jars with insects, a bag full of leaves, or a pocketful of rocks. Meanwhile, you've jotted down notes in your notebook and sketched a few pictures of what you saw. Now it's time to sort through everything.

Set up a place at home where you can work. Ideally, you will want a table where you can spread out your specimens and equipment. Some shelves or cupboards are handy to store things. However, it is not necessary to have a lot of space. A folding table with some boxes underneath will be enough to start. You can upgrade as you go along.

The first order of business is to take care of your specimens. Find appropriate containers, such as small plastic food storage containers or resealable plastic bags. Use labels or tape to identify them. If you have live animals, make sure they have food, water, and ventilation. If you are collecting leaves, you can preserve them by pressing them between the pages of a book. (Wait a couple of weeks to give them time to dry out.)

For closeup study, a sealed jar is a good tool . . . but then let your study subjects go!

You may also put leaves between two pieces of wax paper, put a towel over it, and iron them to seal the paper together.

It's helpful to have a microscope and slides, but don't worry if you don't. There's plenty to see with the naked eye or with a magnifying glass. A small dissection kit can be purchased, or you can assemble one yourself. The basics include scissors, tweezers, a small knife or scalpel, and pointed probes to pull apart delicate areas. When dissecting animals or handling plants, wear fitted, disposable, gloves. Animals can carry diseases, and some plants are poisonous. They could give you a rash, or you could accidentally get the poison in your mouth.

Use a framed box to arrange your discoveries for display.

Think of your work area as a small museum or laboratory. Now you get to decide how to organize it. You might want to keep insects in one place, bird eggs in another, and all your rocks together. Another idea is to organize them by the habitats you found them in. Certain flowers and butterflies might go together, for example. You're the naturalist and it's your lab. It's up to you!

 ## TEXT-DEPENDENT QUESTIONS

1. Why should you avoid wearing bright colors when you are observing nature?

2. Name three things to take in your nature backpack.

3. What are the parts of a dissection kit?

 ## RESEARCH PROJECT

Choose one category in your collection of specimens—leaves, rocks, insects, whatever. Use a field guide or the Internet to outline what you have. Now identify what is likely to exist in your area, but that you are missing.

Tips for Naturalists

bioblitz a short event during which people make notes about the nature in a particular area

conservation the act of preserving or protecting, such as an environment or species

fossil fuels fuel that cannot be renewed, such as oil and gas

rewilding helping land return to its natural state

CHAPTER 4

Further Adventures

Discovering nature takes a lifetime. Most people go outside regularly, but very few take the time to really look around. Those who do are always noticing new things. Their observational skills get better. Bit by bit, they add to their knowledge and understanding of the world around them.

The Role of a Naturalist

Plants and animals do their work in a lot of different environments. So do naturalists! Some people even make a living at it. They may work for national parks, museums, zoos, or aquariums. Several governmental agencies study the environment. They depend on naturalists, biologists, botanists and

Part of discovering nature is helping it, such as at a beach clean-up.

other scientists who understand ecosystems and how they work. One role of a naturalist is to educate other people about what is happening in nature. Naturalists often lead programs that let people explore nature for themselves. They might also organize projects that improve the environment, such as cleaning up a river or beach.

Most naturalists are not professionals. They just want to observe and understand what is happening around them. There are a lot of things to study in nature. Fortunately, there are a lot of people everywhere to help with the project! "Citizen scientists" are just regular people who are interested in nature and the environment. They can help professional scientists by collecting data and making observations about what is happening. They may come up with ideas of what to study. They may also have good ideas of how to conduct research.

A good example of citizen science is the Christmas Bird Count. It began in 1900 and is sponsored by the National Audubon Society. (The Society is named for John Audubon, a famous American naturalist.) The idea of preserving the environment was still new back then. More people wanted to hunt birds over the holidays, not count them. The Audubon Society eventually decided to change this tradition. Now, from mid-December to early January each year, groups of volunteers count the number and types of birds that live in their region. There are more than 2,000 of these groups across the United States. The information helps with **conservation** efforts.

Other citizen scientists can participate in a **bioblitz**. During a bioblitz, people make a record of an area's natural habitat—but they do it fast. Usually, a bioblitz only lasts 24 hours. People focus on a specific area. They find, identify, and count as many different types of plants and animals as possible.

Birdwatchers often gather to make sure everyone spots a species.

Formal scientific studies often focus on areas that are remote or unique. In a bioblitz, people concentrate their efforts in ordinary places. They may study parks, cities, suburbs, or industrial areas. Bioblitzes are held all over the world. They are often sponsored by groups dedicated to the environment. These events help add to scientists' knowledge about an area. They also involve and educate people about their surroundings.

Rewilding

ver the last century, people have started to realize the effect they have on the environment. For example, climate change is mostly caused by humans burning **fossil fuels**. Hotter temperatures throw off the delicate balance in nature. Icebergs melt and fires are more common. All of this puts species at risk.

NATURALIST INTELLIGENCE

Some people are book-smart and some people are street-smart. Other people are nature-smart. Anyone can develop their skills at observing nature, but some people are "naturally" inclined to it. Are you? The more questions you answer with yes, the better your "Naturalist IQ."

1. Are you interested in the survival and health of plants, animals, and ecosystems?

2. Do you tend to see patterns in nature?

3. Do you remember details about what you have observed while being outside, such as the particular look, sound, or smell of something?

4. Do you like to categorize and classify things you observe?

5. Do you notice changes in the environment?

6. Do you notice things that other people often miss?

7. Do you like to read or research about the work of other naturalists?

Nature is as close as your backyard. Discover what new plants you can grow!

Meanwhile, human development has spread to nearly every place on the globe. Roads cut through places that used to be wilderness. People cut down trees to build new houses and buildings. This makes it difficult for animals to move around freely. Large mammals have it particularly bad. They are at great risk all over the world. Elephants, rhinoceroses, tigers, grizzly bears, and many other animals are running out of places to live. As a result, there are fewer and fewer of them.

Fortunately, there are efforts to reverse the damage. Many conservationists support an idea called **rewilding**. This is the process of restoring the land to its natural state. If more areas are natural, it helps plants and animals thrive. The rewilding movement involves three C's: cores, corridors, and carnivores. Cores are like "home base." These are large, undisturbed areas of land where animals can live. Corridors are the hallways and highways. Unlike humans, animals do not like paved roads

Many nature trails are not made by people, but are based on animal movements.

Human rewilding is part of the bigger rewilding effort. It focuses on putting people in touch with nature so they understand how they fit into nature's "big picture." People are attracted to human rewilding for a lot of reasons. Some want to learn wilderness skills, such as hunting and building fires. Other people just want to get away from it all and live "off

the grid." The grid is society, and all that comes with it—from electricity to the Internet. Living off the grid lets people be more self-sufficient. At least for a little while, they can get away from traffic!

with signs. Instead, their corridors are wilderness areas, but they are linked together. They connect the cores and let animals move around without having to leave their habitats. Carnivores are large, meat-eating predators at the top of the food chain. They are needed to help control the populations of smaller animals. Carnivores are at great risk. The cores and corridors are set up to help their populations survive.

In some places, large, undeveloped areas are now being made off-limits to humans so that animals will have enough room. In places where human development has already happened, there are efforts to make the areas more friendly to animals. For example, throughout the United States and Canada, people have begun to put in wildlife crossings. These are natural bridges and pathways that let animals get from one place to another without having to leave their natural environment.

Rewilding efforts don't just help animals. They help people, too. When people take the time to observe what is happening in the natural world, they feel more connected to it. They are more likely to do their part in keeping things running smoothly.

People go to school and work, and they have jobs to do within their families. They also have a place in nature. Knowing more about it helps them understand where they fit in relation to everything else. Discovering nature is just one part of discovering ourselves.

Pack a picnic, gather some friends, and discover the great outdoors!

TEXT-DEPENDENT QUESTIONS

1. Where are three places naturalists work?
2. What is a bioblitz?
3. What are the "three C's" of rewilding?

 ## RESEARCH PROJECT

Find out ways that citizen scientists are at work in your area. How could you be part of a bioblitz, a bird count, or rewilding efforts?

The Environmental Movement

FIND OUT MORE

WEBSITES

www.backyardnature.net/index.html
This site, from naturalist Jim Conrad, has tips on getting the most from nature explorations as well as information on the different things found in nature.

www.exploringnature.org/
From animals to astronomy, this site has information about many aspects of nature.

www.discoverlife.org/
For advanced naturalists, this site has tools for identifying species and reporting findings.

BOOKS

George, Jean Craighead. *Pocket Guide to the Outdoors*. New York: Penguin Group, 2009.

Leslie, Clare Walker. *The Nature Connection: An Outdoor Workbook for Kids, Families, and Classrooms*. North Adams, Mass.: Storey Publishing, 2010.

Rothman, Julia. *Nature Anatomy: The Curious Parts and Pieces of the Natural World*. North Adams, Mass.: Storey Publishing, 2015.

bushcraft wilderness skills, named for the remote bush country of Australia

camouflage a pattern or disguise in clothing designed to make it blend in to the surroundings

conservation the act of preserving or protecting, such as an environment or species

ecosystem the habitats of species and the ways that species interact with each other

friction the resistance that happens when two surfaces rub together

insulation protection from something, such as extreme hot or cold

layering adding layers of clothing to stay warm and removing layers to cool off.

rewilding returning to a more natural state

synthetic manmade, often to imitate a natural material

traction the grip or contact that an object has with another surface

wake the waves produced by the movement of a boat

INDEX

Amazon Basin 9, 17

animals 8, 11, 19, 20, 22, 41,43

apps 30

Audobon, John 39

backpack 30, 31

binoculars 31

bioblitz 39, 40

Brazil 17

Christmas Bird Count 39

citizen scientists 38

Clark, William 12, 13

clothing 27, 28, 29

collecting specimens 31, 32, 33, 34

Darwin, Charles 13

field guide 24, 30

food 32

greater prairie chicken 8

Hamerstrom, Frances 7, 8, 9

human nature 14

Industrial Revolution 13

insects 7, 29, 31

Lewis, Meriwether 12, 13

Linneaus, Carl 12

museum 7, 35

naming plants and animals 23, 24

National Audobon Society 39

naturalists 8, 9, 11, 14, 18, 37, 38, 40, 41

nocturnal animals 20

notetaking 21, 22

photography 22

plants 18, 20

rewilding 40, 41, 42

shoes 29

Wisconsin 8

PHOTO CREDITS

ABOUT THE AUTHOR

Diane Bailey has written about 50 nonfiction books for kids and teens, on topics ranging from science to sports to celebrities. Diane also works as a freelance editor, helping authors who write novels for children and young adults. She has two sons and two dogs, and lives in Kansas.